W9-BMR-810

Hearing

by Helen Frost

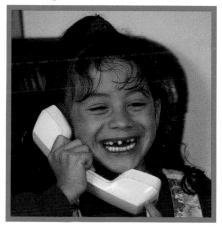

Consulting Editor: Gail Saunders-Smith, Ph.D.

Consultant: Eric H. Chudler, Ph.D.
Research Associate Professor
Department of Anesthesiology
University of Washington, Seattle

Pebble Books

an imprint of Capstone Press
Mankato, Minnesota

Pebble Books are published by Capstone Press
818 North Willow Street, Mankato, Minnesota 56001
http://www.capstone-press.com

Library of Congress Cataloging-in-Publication Data
Frost, Helen, 1949–
    Hearing/by Helen Frost.
    p. cm.—(The Senses)
    Includes bibliographical references and index.
    Summary: Simple text and photographs present the sense of hearing and how
it works.
    ISBN 0-7368-0382-3
    1. Hearing—Juvenile literature. [1. Hearing. 2. Ear. 3. Senses and sensation.]
I. Title. II. Series: Frost, Helen, 1949– The senses.
QP462.2.F76 2000
612.8′5—dc21   99-18965
                                                                                                              CIP

Note to Parents and Teachers

The Senses series supports national science standards for units
related to behavioral science. This book describes and illustrates
the sense of hearing. The photographs support early readers in
understanding the text. This book also introduces early readers to
subject-specific vocabulary words, which are defined in the Words
to Know section. Early readers may need assistance to read some
words and to use the Table of Contents, Words to Know, Read
More, Internet Sites, and Index/Word List sections of the book.

Table of Contents

4

Hearing is one of
your five senses. You
use your ears to hear.

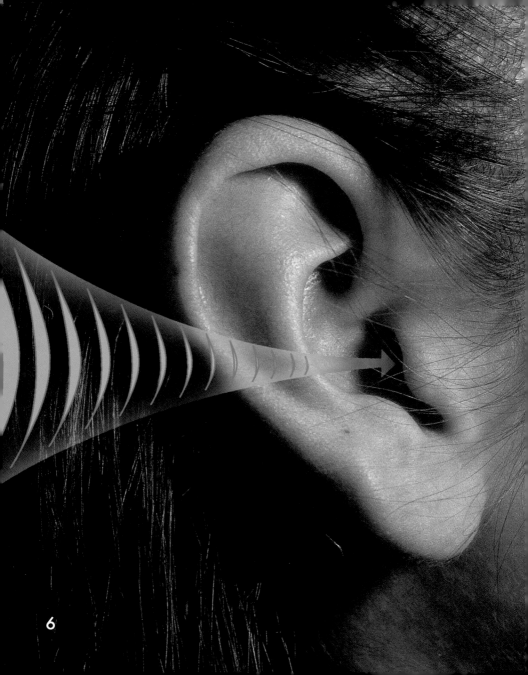

Your outer ear catches sound waves. The sound waves travel down a tunnel inside your ear.

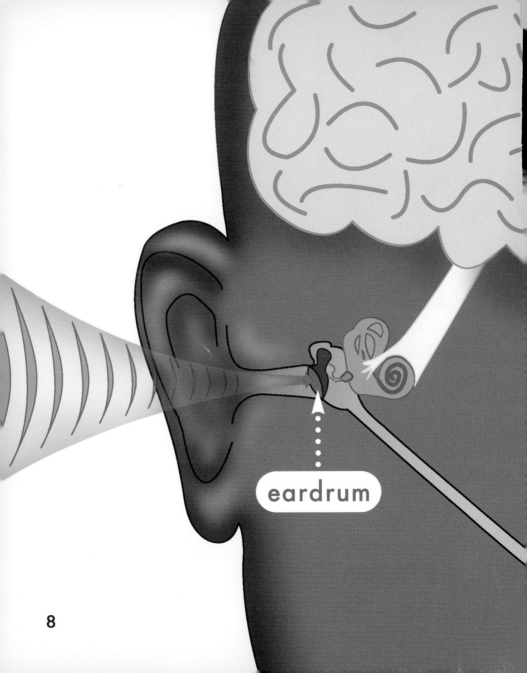

eardrum

8

The sound waves hit your eardrum. Your eardrum vibrates. The vibrations make nerve signals.

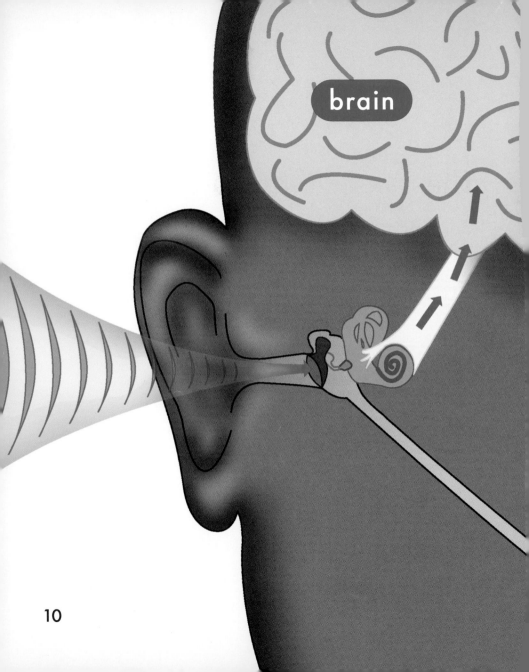

brain

The nerve signals travel to your brain. Your brain understands what you hear.

You can hear loud
sounds. An airplane
makes a loud sound.

You can hear soft
sounds. A whisper
is a soft sound.

You can hear high sounds. A whistle makes a high sound.

You can hear low
sounds. A drum
makes a low sound.

Many sounds together
make a new sound.

Words to Know

brain—the body part inside your head that controls your body; your brain understands what your ears hear.

eardrum—a thin skin inside your ear; the eardrum vibrates when sound waves hit it.

outer ear—the part of your ear that is on the outside of your head

sense—a way of knowing about things around you; hearing is one of your five senses; seeing, smelling, tasting, and touching are your other senses.

signal—a message; sensors in your ears send signals to your brain.

sound wave—a wave or vibration that can be heard

vibration—a fast movement back and forth

Read More

Ballard, Carol. *How Do Our Ears Hear?* How Our Bodies Work. Austin, Texas: Raintree Steck-Vaughn, 1998.

Frost, Helen. *Your Senses.* The Senses. Mankato, Minn.: Pebble Books, 2000.

Pluckrose, Henry Arthur. *Listening and Hearing.* Senses. Austin, Texas: Raintree Steck-Vaughn, 1998.

Internet Sites

Hearing Experiments
http://faculty.washington.edu/chudler/chhearing.html

How Your Ear Works
http://KidsHealth.org/kid/somebody/ear.html

Sense of Hearing
http://www.yucky.com/body/index.ssf?/systems/hearing/

The Sound Site
http://www.smm.org/sound/nocss/top.html

Index/Word List

brain, 11
ear, 5, 7
eardrum, 9
hear, 5, 11, 13, 15,
 17, 19
high, 17
loud, 13
low, 19
nerve signals,
 9, 11
outer ear, 7

senses, 5
soft, 15
sound, 13, 15, 17,
 19, 21
sound waves,
 7, 9
travel, 7, 11
tunnel, 7
understands, 11
vibrations, 9

Word Count: 107
Early-Intervention Level: 14

Editorial Credits
Mari C. Schuh, editor; Timothy Halldin, cover designer; Kevin T. Kes and
 Linda Clavel, illustrators; Kimberly Danger, photo researcher

Photo Credits
David F. Clobes, 6
Index Stock Imagery/M. Bednar, 12
Photo Network/Myrleen Cate, 1
Photophile/Jeff Greenberg, cover
Shaffer Photography/James L. Shaffer, 4, 18
Transparencies, Inc./Ginger Wagoner, 14
Unicorn Stock Photos/Russell R. Grundke, 16; Dennis MacDonald, 20